QUICK START GUIDE

NARCISSISTIC ABUSE RECOVERY

MEREDITH MILLER

CONTENTS

INTRODUCTION

So you recently discovered that you're in a relationship with a narcissist or psychopath . . .

You are not alone. You're one of millions and millions of people who have been through narcissistic abuse. Fortunately, you figured out what was going on. Most people still don't know what's happening to them. Some people spend decades or even a whole lifetime in it, which is a tragedy.

I created this *Quick Start Guide* to help you get started on your recovery journey after narcissistic abuse with the most simplified, basic, tactical information that you need to know to get the ball rolling. In this mini book, you'll learn about the first three most essential steps that you can take right now to start moving forward and transforming your life.

It doesn't have to be like this forever, even though it might feel like that right now. Until we develop awareness of a problem, we can't fix it. Now that you're aware of narcissistic abuse, you're at the precipice of an opportunity to change your life.

I personally believe that narcissistic and psychopathic abuse is the most devastating social issue facing human beings in our individual and collective stories.

It's not hard to see that there are many problems in our society, families and interpersonal relationships. Most of these problems are a downstream result of the lack of conscience that allows some people to behave in ways that leave a trail of death and destruction everywhere they go.

While the more overt form of narcissistic abuse is more obviously abusive, the covert form is far more dangerous because it's disguised as good. For that reason, it can go undetected and the damage can reach so much farther before anyone sees what's happening. It can easily be rationalized through plausible deniability, making it very difficult to show others the truth.

That's actually the worst part for the survivor—when no one believes you. The abuse is traumatizing, for sure. But the part that causes the post-trauma is when no one is there for you. If you feel isolated in your perception of reality, then you feel utterly alone in the world. That's the part that causes the most damage, and that's exactly what covert narcissistic abuse does to an extreme.

Whether you've been through a more overt or covert form of abuse, you'll find that the information in this book applies because the recovery steps are the same.

I have some quick reflections to share with you before you read about the first three steps of the recovery after narcissistic abuse.

By now, you likely suspect that you are in (or were in) a relationship of narcissistic abuse. Somehow you stumbled upon me or another expert in the field online or maybe someone specifically mentioned a keyword to you like "narcissist" or "psychopath" and you went down the rabbit hole looking for more information.

Discovering that it's a thing and it happens to a lot of people was probably incredibly relieving, albeit also devastating. I encourage you not to stop there. That's actually the first point where people get stuck.

Sometimes people confuse the relief of new awareness with healing. This keeps people trapped in repetition cycles of the same old toxic dynamics, while their sense of powerlessness, helplessness and resentment grows over time and things get much, much worse.

That doesn't have to be your future.

As a caveat, while reading this book and walking through your healing journey in general, I recommend you not worry about which personality disorder your abuser has or if they have a full-blown personality disorder.

While those can be helpful keyword terms for independent researching purposes, the obsession with finding an official diagnosis can become a form of mental masturbation, distracting you from your healing journey—and worse yet, adding on a whole other layer of self-doubt and confusion.

Also, don't let people gaslight you into thinking that you cannot decide for yourself if a person is abusive to you. People who are cut from the same cloth as your abuser (and their enablers) will tell you that you're not qualified or credentialed to have an opinion on these matters. They will try to make you doubt yourself and your perception of reality, which is more of what you've already experienced in an emotionally abusive relationship.

You'll need to learn to be the authority of your life and

stop outsourcing that position unless you want to be a prime candidate for more abusers. You do not need to be a therapist to recognize and understand abuse.

So don't get hung up on needing a label as a psychiatrist or therapist would diagnose a patient. And by the way, many of them have no idea how to recognize the signs of narcissistic abuse!

Clients often tell me that they spent years in therapy but the mental health professional was never able to identify what happened. Instead they were told to focus on communication and forgiveness. That's literally the worst advice a person could give a victim of narcissistic abuse.

I've even had clients who are therapists and psychologists (some with PhDs!) who told me that they didn't recognize when it was happening to them. They were never taught about narcissistic abuse in their training programs.

When dealing with abuse, I recommend you focus on identifying and labeling the toxic patterns of behavior. This is where you'll notice the alarming lack of conscience.

At the core, it's a spiritual disease—a disorder of the conscience. This is essentially the reason why some people use, abuse and mistreat others.

It's important to know what's not okay for you, no matter what personality disorder the person has or if they have a full-blown personality disorder. It will serve you greatly in the future to be able to identify the behaviors instead of getting disoriented by your feelings (or other people's feelings) for the person. You can use whatever terms you prefer.

What most matters is that you identified harmful patterns of behavior and now you know it's not normal or healthy.

For the purpose of simplification in this book, I will mostly use the word "narcissist" to describe the self-absorbed person with a spiritual disorder of the conscience who brought pain and suffering into your life through abuse and manipulation.

You may have encountered narcissistic abuse in an intimate relationship, friendship, family member, co-worker, employee, boss, business associate, neighbor, etc. Most people start waking up to this awareness through an intimate relationship with a narcissist.

The patterns of abuse and the destruction that abusers bring into the lives of their targets is eerily similar. Of course, there are nuances based on the kind of relationship you had, the length of that relationship and the uniqueness of each individual.

Maybe you've already noticed, from talking with others or reading comments online, just how similar the patterns of narcissistic abuse are across the globe—regardless of culture, country, race, socio-economic status and gender.

Some people wonder if they all read the same manual. It sure seems like it, but that wouldn't be possible.

After several years of contemplation, I've come to believe that this phenomenon reveals the spiritual nature of narcissistic abuse. *They're all serving the same master.* Whether they're religious, spiritual or atheist doesn't matter. What they all have in common is that they're driven by a negative energy force—call it whatever you like.

There's so much information out there on narcissistic abuse that it can be overwhelming at first. It's hard to know where to start and what to do next. This guide is going to help you get the clarity to cut through all the confusion.

Information is helpful, and it's good to learn new information. However, too much information can be paralyzing. You probably desperately want to find the clarity to start taking action forward. I'm going to show you, in three simple steps, what you can do to start feeling better right now.

If you want to transform your life, you'll need to take new action. That's what this *Quick Start Guide for Narcissistic Abuse Recovery* is about. I'm going to give you the first three action steps to take, while walking you through that process like a friend who has been down that road before.

While it's understandable that you feel a sense of urgency to get better and put all of that suffering behind you, it's also important to understand that recovery is a process. It will take time and it will be worth your efforts. One day you can look back at where you are right now in deep gratitude that you've come so far.

This book will not heal you and it doesn't contain a magic pill to make it all go away. But the good news is that it's possible to recover and you can do it! I believe in you.

By putting these three steps into action, you can get unstuck and start moving forward, out of the inertia and overwhelm where you find yourself right now.

Most importantly, as you put these steps into action, you'll start to believe in yourself and in your ability to transform your life because you'll see the results.

I'm sending you a big hug!

Meredith Miller

Coach & Author
Inner Integration

MENTAL NINJA MINDSET

When you're facing an enormous task, it's easy to get overwhelmed and feel like nothing is ever going to change. That's where a mental ninja mindset is essential.

You've got to start small to go BIG! Don't get down on yourself, looking at the long road of recovery ahead and wanting it all to just be done. You'll get there, step by step, if you keep putting in the effort. Right now—at the beginning of your journey and starting from Ground Zero—you need to focus on each step in front of you and keep taking steps forward.

When I go to Teotihuacán and climb up (or back down) the steep, narrow stairs of the pyramids, I know not to look too far ahead because I'll get dizzy and scared. It's overwhelming. My knees start shaking. I start to feel anxious and paralyzed, unable to take another step. It's hard to catch my breath. That's when I have to remind myself to focus on my feet and each next step.

In scary and overwhelming moments like these in life, the best way forward is to focus on *one step at a time*.

Everything big that you build in your life starts somewhere small. That's normal and that's okay! Don't be ashamed of where you are right now.

Firstly, you're not alone. There are millions of other people in a very similar place.

Secondly, if you can't accept where you are, that will make it difficult to move forward. Your inner GPS needs to know where you are in order to guide you to your destination. While it keeps the destination as the goal, it shows you each next step, one step at a time. The longest journeys can seem endless when you just want to get there. But when you focus instead on each next step, before you know it, you'll be there.

Another important thing is to stop comparing yourself to anyone else. When you've been triangulated so much by abusive people, you might have developed a tendency to compare yourself ruthlessly to others and then feel a deep sense of shame about yourself in comparison. Remind yourself that's *their* journey, not yours. You've probably already been through enough comparisons from the narcissist to last you a lifetime. This is one of the ways that people can end up hurting themselves in a similar way that they were hurt by others.

From now on, the only comparisons you want to make are looking back at who you were yesterday, last week, last month, last year and so on. The only person you're in competition with is your past self. This will help you to realize how far you've come, each step of the way, so you can celebrate your progress and growth. This is not an exercise in beating yourself up!

Progress is uncomfortable. Can you let yourself get comfortable with uncomfortable?

If there were a magic pill with no side effects that you could take to be done with this already—to be miraculously healed 100%—well, pretty much everyone would want to take it! Unfortunately that pill doesn't exist.

This self-healing journey after narcissistic abuse is long and hard. It's full of ups and downs, and you will have to face things about yourself that you might not want to see. I can also tell you that it's totally worth it! It's worth every discomfort, difficulty and challenge along the way because in the process, you'll be growing, becoming a new and improved version of yourself.

You didn't deserve what happened to you. It wasn't your fault. However, you are the one who can do something about it now.

The only other option is to sit around in the muck and feel horrible, complaining endlessly about the people who hurt you and what happened to you, while time passes and nothing changes. That might feel good at first, but you won't get better if you stay stuck in the victimhood.

Victim consciousness is a stage we all go through after narcissistic abuse—it's not a life sentence.

Staying stuck in the disempowerment is the easy button, and it's one of two options that you have right now.

Sitting around and complaining is a lot easier than taking action. The more challenging option is to put in the work, to get messy and uncomfortable, to face the truth and set yourself free. This is definitely the more difficult option, which is why it's so worth it and also why most people don't do it. Anything valuable in life is rare and requires work to obtain.

If you want to have a different life than the one you're currently living, you need to be willing to do things you've never done before.

This journey of recovery requires work. No one will

hand it to you. No one will rescue you. No one will do it for you. I know, it's a burden and it sucks. But for whatever reason, that's what happened and now you have the opportunity to transform your life.

Your choices are where you'll find your power.

Rescue fantasies and hitting the easy button will only delay your progress, perhaps landing you in more problems and devastating experiences.

While it may be hard to believe from where you're sitting right now, I can promise you that if you're willing to do the work, you can have a much better life than you ever imagined possible. I know this for a fact because I experienced it myself and I've helped many others go through this transformation as well.

Consistency is key. Inconsistent efforts will lead to inconsistent results.

If you want to see results, you've got to work on yourself and your recovery every day. You're going to have to fight the self-sabotage and self-destructive voices in your head telling you to give up, to stop trying, to mask the feelings with addictions, distractions and other forms of escapism.

There will be moments when you want to give up and never try again. It's precisely in those moments when you need to summon up your desire to keep going. Think about what matters and why it matters in order to motivate yourself to get back up. This is how you develop grit.

Now that you've got a quick introduction to the mental ninja mindset, it's time to walk through the first three tactical steps of the recovery process together. You can come back to this information as often as you need to, whenever you want to inspire yourself and get motivated again.

ONE
STEP 1—EDUCATE YOURSELF

This is when you do research. By now, you're probably already feeling the ravenous hunger for information about what you went through and the kinds of people who do such things.

You're likely already trying to discover everything you can about terms like narcissistic abuse, emotional abuse, coercive control, narcissistic personality disorder, antisocial personality disorder, narcissists, covert narcissists, psychopaths, sociopaths, toxic people, gaslighting, blame-shifting, triangulation, cognitive dissonance, trauma bonding, and all the other lingo.

This first step is also referred to as going down the rabbit hole, because just like Alice in Wonderland, your reality is about to change in ways you never imagined.

The discovery of all these topics under the umbrella of narcissistic abuse is going to help you shift your perspective about what happened as you weave together all the pieces into a new story.

Depending on your learning style and preferences, you might be more drawn to watching videos, listening to podcasts, reading articles or books, scrolling through social media posts, joining online support groups, etc. If you're really industrious, you might be doing all of the above.

You're educating yourself so you can start to label toxic behaviors and understand better what was happening to you.

There's a lot of talk nowadays about not judging or labeling people and things. While there is some truth to that, it's also very important during this first phase of your recovery that you learn the terms to help you name what happened as well as the specific manipulative behaviors that you witnessed.

It's also important to put the label on the narcissist (psychopath, manipulator, abuser, etc.) so you can let yourself off the hook and stop trying to fix the unfixable. Again, this isn't about needing a diagnosis. It's about finding the language that helps you label the abuser, which reminds you how dangerous that person is for your health, sanity and wellbeing.

You'll have to repeat it to yourself over and over for your subconscious mind to shift the old perception.

This labeling practice might feel very uncomfortable if you have a belief system about not judging. Keep in mind that being judgmental and having good judgment are two different things.

For example, the stove is hot. This is a judgment that helps you avoid burning yourself. It's not judgmental—it's just a fact. When you say it's hot outside today, that's also a judgment because you're making a distinction between hot and cold or somewhere in between. However, it's not judgmental to say it's hot outside—it's just a fact. When you label the abuser, think of the hot stove analogy or the hot day. It is what it is.

It's also important to understand that we often don't learn lessons the first time, even when it's a painful experience. You can teach your kids not to touch the hot stove. Yet they often touch it despite your warnings and sometimes they'll even touch it *again* despite their own painful experience. Adults aren't so different. As humans, we often learn lessons the hard way—painfully—until we finally get it and stop going back for more.

The label helps train your mind to stop going back for more abuse and pain. You'll need to repeat it to yourself many times and you'll probably forget some things more than once. As Zig Ziglar said, "Repetition is the mother of learning, the father of action."

Now that you're educating yourself on narcissistic abuse, you're currently in the process of developing better judgment of people and their behaviors in order to avoid a replay of those painful experiences.

The more you learn about abusive and manipulative behaviors, the better prepared you'll be for filtering out these kinds of people and situations much quicker. This is why it's so important to educate yourself.

In your research, I highly recommend that you learn about covert abuse. It's far more tricky to recognize because it's very subtle and disguised as good. In this category are the covert narcissists (who are more passive) and the psychopaths (who are the most charming, calculated and meticulous predators). The most sophisticated ones make you believe that they're helping you, while they're actually destroying you.

Something that I learned along my own journey in the recovery process is that each time you fall into a new abuser, they're usually more covert than the last one. Your awareness and detection skills will need to keep evolving in order to stay ahead of the game.

Later down the road of your recovery, you'll need to delve deeper into your research in order to recognize your own neurological and psychological programming from childhood that set you up to normalize this kind of treatment from others.

But not yet.

In this early stage of education, you're first working to understand the *external* truth about what happened and who the other person is. However, you might already be noticing how some things reminded you of childhood. It's okay to note those insights on the sidebar for now.

While not everyone that ends up in an abusive relationship or situation as an adult had abusive parents, in many cases this is true. In other cases it was something different that led to similar coping mechanisms.

Sometimes it was the neglect of an alcoholic or addict parent, or perhaps one who was physically or mentally ill. Other cases could involve factors such as poverty, war or natural disasters that affected the parents' ability to be present for the children in order to meet their needs and take their feelings seriously.

But for right now, it would be too much to unpack your childhood since you first have so much to sort out from a recent abusive circumstance as an adult.

It's good to mentally note that your early life subconscious and neurological programming will continue to sabotage you, no matter how much you consciously learn about abusers and their tactics. You'll need to deal with that eventually if you want to truly set yourself free.

Right now in the early moments of self-healing, it's just one step at a time, one foot in front of the other.

The more you're able to understand and label the people who hurt you and their hurtful actions, the greater sense of relief you will have at this stage. Once you realize this is a thing that manipulative people do—and there are very predictable behavioral patterns of abuse and manipulation—then you don't have to obsess so much about what happened.

The obsessive rumination happens when your mind is trying to make sense of things and set the story straight while you're still not fully sure what happened.

The more you're able to articulate what happened, the less you'll feel lost in a desperate sense of confusion. Armed with the words to describe your experience, you won't have to keep wasting so much energy in the mental fight, defending yourself to the narcissist or to your own inner voice.

That means you'll be able to reduce the amount of rumination so you can start to free up some of your mental and emotional energy in order to focus on the next steps.

The educational process can go on as long as you choose. It could go on endlessly, and indeed some people stay stuck here. It's great to always be learning. However, the difference is that when you're stuck on the first step, it's because you're only gathering information and not putting it into action.

The only way to move forward is by making the decision to do so when you're ready. That doesn't mean you'll never learn more again. It simply means that you're choosing to start making new choices by applying the information you've learned so far.

Knowledge isn't power—it's only potential power. Like

a ball at rest, it needs a force to start moving. Knowledge becomes power when we put it into real life practice. Then it matures into wisdom. That process requires taking action.

This shift into action will require mobilizing yourself out of the frozen state where you feel like you're just spinning endlessly in information.

What happens if you don't educate yourself?

- You'll keep accepting manipulative, abusive people in your life because you haven't learned how to recognize and identify the red flags before you get hurt.
- You'll keep getting drained and destroyed by energy vampires and soul crushers because you won't realize what they're doing until it's too late.
- You'll keep jumping from one abusive relationship or situation to the next, thinking each time that you finally found something good—until the sharp left turn when a person turns out to be another shade of narcissist.
- You'll continually feel betrayed and deceived again by the people in your life.
- You'll torment yourself asking why this keeps happening to you and what you did to deserve it. You didn't deserve it. It's just that you didn't see it, so you couldn't protect yourself from letting it happen again.
- You'll feel like there's no escape from this endless cycle of repetition compulsion, so you'll

fall deeper into a state of learned helplessness and spiritual bankruptcy with ongoing shame spirals.

- The confusion, brain fog and dissociation will continue, making it hard to think clearly, to remember things or to be present in your body. That makes you an ideal target for another abuser.

What happens if you stay stuck at this step?

If you make the effort to educate yourself and learn about narcissistic abuse, you'll know some things—maybe a lot of things. But if you don't move on to the next step, nothing will change after your initial sense of relief.

You could get caught indefinitely in the obsession with getting more and more information. It's like chasing the dragon, looking for the same high of relief that you got when you first discovered information about narcissistic abuse. But it won't be the same.

You'll still feel awful. Maybe you won't be as confused as before, but you'll still be obsessed with what happened. You'll feel like you just can't get out of that habit. At this point, you'll be drowning yourself in the depression and resentment or stewing in the anger that abusive people caused you and keep causing you. This can become an ongoing cycle, going back and forth between depression and anger.

Over time, you'll likely develop a negative and pessimistic view of your life or about men/women. This can turn you into a toxic person that healthy people don't want to be around.

You'll develop limiting belief systems like: "all men/women are terrible," "no one loves me because I'm unloveable," or "I'm too old / fat / busy being a single parent, etc."

You'll isolate yourself in a defensive posture, which feels safer but blocks healthy connection.

You'll convince yourself that you're fine but the loneliness will mutate into a longing and craving for someone—anyone—to distract you from this feeling. Cue the next abusive relationship or situation.

You'll be living in survival mode, highly reactive to the world around you, always on guard for the next attack, and unable to trust anyone or anything.

You'll feel like a powerless victim of life because you don't see that you have choices.

You might vow to never date or open your heart again because it's just too dangerous. Then you can become hard and rigid, blocking your own happiness and ability to thrive.

You'll stay in other relationships that are not healthy for you and you'll likely keep getting hurt by the same kinds of people over and over again, while hoping they will change. The only difference is now you're able to label things with the vocabulary that you learned. But you'll still feel powerless because you haven't set any new boundaries or restored your agency through the power of choice.

You'll keep leaning into more abusers and getting more of the same results like devastation, shame, low self-worth and self-esteem, loss of integrity, self-trust and identity.

You don't have to stay stuck here. But you will need to mentally override the neurological state of collapse and shutdown ("freeze" response) in order to mobilize yourself to take action. This will require mental and spiritual fortitude. If you feel like you can't, you'll need to find a why—a reason to get back up and start moving forward.

Keep going and don't give up on yourself! You are the one who can rescue yourself from this life predicament.

Your future self is counting on you.

Your kids (or future kids) are counting on you to break this pattern and make new choices so they can have a better future too.

Even if you don't have kids, your healing process can send positive ripples out to the world around you. Your liberation can inspire another person to liberate themselves.

————

Step 1 Recommended Homework

What are the top 8-10 things you've learned so far in your research about narcissistic abuse? These can be terms, concepts, lessons, insights, realizations, etc.

What do you most need to educate yourself about right now? Be specific about the top 3-5 things that you want to learn more about.

You can keep updating your answers to these questions as you check in with yourself periodically.

TWO
STEP 2—NO CONTACT

Executing No Contact with the narcissists in your life is the most important boundary that you can set in order to protect your health and sanity. This might even be the first boundary that you learn.

No Contact is when you cut off the narcissist.

This means you completely end all communication and connection with them. It's best to block and delete them from the phone, WhatsApp, email, Messenger, and all social media. First of all, this prevents you from reaching out to them or seeing what they post online. Secondly, if you leave even one channel of communication open, they will likely contact you.

That contact can set you way back in your recovery, whether you respond or not.

It might not be today. It could be months down the road, just when you're starting to feel significantly better. Suddenly you get contacted and your nervous system gets hijacked. You're instantly catapulted backward in your recovery journey, re-living the pain of your past all over again.

It's easy to think that you don't have to completely block them. You could be telling yourself that you'll just not respond if they contact you. This is usually coming from a sense of morbid curiosity where you kind of want to see what they have to say or what they will do. Maybe you even want to know that they still miss you. Or perhaps you just want to see what they're up to on social media.

This is playing with fire and you will likely get burned.

I've seen it happen over and over again in my own life and in others' lives. The only alternative to that downward spiral is to set yourself up for success by going No Contact.

If you leave any doors open, the narcissist will creep back in before you realize it and more harm will be done. You could even be your worst enemy, impulsively reaching out to them in order to calm the intense anxiety of withdrawal.

Why is No Contact important?

No Contact protects you against further abuse from any current or past abusers in your life. It's not easy to do, however, it's necessary if you want to create the peace and protection that you'll need in order to move forward in the healing journey.

No Contact is also the start of reprogramming your nervous system to recognize abuse and set boundaries around abusive behavior.

It's similar to the reason why an alcoholic or addict needs to go completely abstinent from the substance in order to reset.

No Contact is the way you start training yourself to

reduce your tolerance to abuse. If you're allowing abusive people in your life, you're training your nervous system to normalize that treatment so it will keep automatically seeking more of the same, even when you know how to recognize the red flags.

Eventually, through training yourself to set these boundaries, your nervous system will automatically catch on and it will be a lot easier. Instead of being drawn to abusive types, feeling obsessed with them in a way that makes it hard to let go, you'll become repulsed by them. You'll eventually develop an allergy to that kind of behavior.

As long as you're in contact with an abuser and accepting their abuse, your nervous system will keep recognizing abuse as normal.

As a human being, you're also a mammal, with a biological imperative to form social connections with others of our species. Connection is integral to our spiritual, physical and mental health.

That biological drive to connect is probably stronger than your desire to know the truth and set boundaries that protect you.

When your primary connections in life are with abusers, it will be very difficult to cut them off because you don't have anyone else. The isolation and loneliness triggers your neurological defense system, which reads disconnection as a life threat.

This makes sense when we think of our earlier human lifestyles. Isolation meant certain death because there was protection in the numbers of the tribe.

This is why people often sacrifice the truth for connection with the herd, even when the herd is moving toward the slaughterhouse. It's the same reason why people cling to an abusive family or other social systems.

Connection is necessary but it's only beneficial when those are healthy relationships.

Going No Contact is like overriding your biological programming that wants you to stay in connection for survival. Your nervous system is seeking connection and this is very dangerous when dealing with abusive people.

In relationships with narcissists, those connections are actually damaging to your health and sanity instead of restorative to your homeostasis like healthy connections.

Even when you're not consciously aware of it, your nervous system is communicating with the nervous systems of other people near you and reading for cues of safety and threat. That's called neuroception. This is why your environment has such a huge impact on your health and well-being.

It requires enormous strength of spirit to take this step and trust that you'll find healthier people to connect with down the road. In the meanwhile, a pet (particularly another mammal) can be a helpful surrogate connection—especially for those of us who have had to brave the wild alone for a while after discovering that we were surrounded by a tribe of narcissists and their enablers.

I want to urge some caution around relying on narcissistic abuse support groups online. It can be helpful to read other stories and see how similar it all is to what you went through. However, in those support groups there's also a lot of commiseration among people who are venting and sharing information but not taking action to heal and transform themselves. You'll probably feel like that environment is holding you back when you outgrow those habits and connections, and want to start moving forward in your recovery.

If you don't have a personal support system of friends and family, then you could decide to create a network of professionals who you trust to help you through the process and bridge the gap between the isolation and new connections.

Feeling connected and supported is important. However the only person who can take the action to set and maintain the boundary of No Contact is you. Every time you practice going No Contact with an abuser, it makes it easier when another one shows up or when you suddenly realize someone else who has been in your life for a while is cut from that same cloth.

When the shocking, sharp left turn happens in a new or old relationship that seemed to be going just fine until that point, you're more likely to draw the line and set the boundary because you're developing the mental fortitude to override your biological impulse to remain in contact with the abuser.

You're becoming a mental ninja!

How to do No Contact

If you don't live with the narcissist, you can execute No Contact by simply blocking them from all possible methods of communication.

This includes not answering the door if they show up where you live or work. That might also mean notifying neighbors, building security, family, friends, etc. to not respond if they should hear from the narcissist.

If you're dealing with a bonafide narcissist, psychopath or sociopath, they will likely reach out to your social network in an effort to get back in contact with you. They will go to extreme lengths to try to get a reaction out of you because they're furious that you cut off their supply source.

Keep in mind that it may not be immediately if they have other sources of narcissistic supply to tide them over while they come up with a plan.

No Contact also means rejecting any gifts or mail sent to you by the narcissist and/or their flying monkeys (enablers). I don't recommend returning the gifts or mail, since the narcissist will perceive it as a form of contact, which continues to feed them narcissistic supply and encourages them to keep coming back for more. The trash bin or a donation center is usually the best option.

No Contact also means throwing away all the paraphernalia.

That means the love letters, photos, sweatshirts, gifts, etc. that the narcissist gave you. I recommend getting rid of all correspondence that you had—unless you share kids with them, since you could need this information for court proceedings. In that case, start a computer file somewhere for all the correspondence that takes place with your ex regarding your children. Document, document, document and most importantly be sure that you are acting in 100% integrity with yourself and the law. Narcissists love to use your transgressions against you in the legal system, so don't give them any fodder.

No Contact also includes not stalking their social media accounts or trying to get information through third parties. Just stay away from all of that if you want to set yourself up for success.

People often ask if they should let the narcissist know that it's over and why. This is up to you. Just keep in mind that you're not dealing with a regular person and nothing you say will go over well.

You're probably looking for closure and wanting to do the decent human thing. But there will always be a negative reaction and the narcissist will block all possible roads to closure.

When you try to end it, they'll work harder to get a reaction out of you, and you could fall into the trap. When they provoke you to react to something they say or do, this could keep you in contact if you aren't able to hold the boundary. They *will* test the boundary one way or another.

If you chose to let them know, it's usually best to write a text that is short, clear, definitive, non-inflammatory, unemotional and direct, such as:

"Thank you for the time we shared together. This is not what I want and it's time for me to move on. Wishing you all the best."

Don't list the reasons and explanations for why you're leaving, no matter how badly you want to tell them all the ways they hurt you. Simply convey that it's over and imagine you're delivering this news with the same tone as if you were telling someone that you ate cereal for breakfast. No big deal. Nothing emotional.

Manipulative people see explanations as an opportunity for negotiation. That will keep the circular conversations going, putting your mind through the spin cycle yet again and draining all your energy that you could be directing to your recovery process.

If they ask for reasons why, don't respond to the invitation to keep negotiating. That is the opportune time to block them from further contact. They got the message you sent but they're not going to let it end.

Even if they say something mean, that doesn't mean they're done with you. They will keep going at you until they get a reaction.

They are addicted to narcissistic supply. As HG Tudor says, the negative form of "fuel" is even more valuable to them. If you don't block them, at some point your self-discipline and mental strength will waver. Then you'll end up falling in the trap by reacting. They know how to push your buttons to extract your emotional energy, so remove the buttons from their access.

If they react negatively, you might think they're having a hard time but they actually enjoy this. Any contact you give them is like giving them a sense of significance. Their worst fear is insignificance. That's why No Contact is so devastating to them.

I highly recommend not ending it in person because that opens you up to the possibility of physical and/or psychological violence, or at the very least more confusion and self-doubt that could cause you to go back on your decision. This is especially precarious if you have chemistry with the narcissist. Your mind is probably not strong enough at this point to resist the intensity of that pull.

If you live with the narcissist, your extraction process is more complicated but not impossible. Remember there is always a way out!

You might currently be financially dependent on the narcissist and unable to leave immediately.

That means you first need a plan of action for your financial independence. You might need to check into job prospects, new housing possibilities, purchasing a vehicle, getting some training, moving in with family temporarily, etc. That plan can take some time, depending on your circumstances. As long as you have a plan and you're taking steps in that direction, you'll get there!

All of your efforts in this plan of escape must be kept secret from the narcissist otherwise you risk the opportunity for them to sabotage it all.

Do not underestimate the narcissist's ability to sabotage you from leaving.

You'll want to move while they're at work, traveling, out for an extended period of time, etc. When they come back, you're simply gone and there was no confrontation.

If they never leave the house for a long enough period of time, you ought to consider having a chaperone (or more) there as a witness and incentive for them to be on their best behavior.

You might choose to leave a note, send an email or text *after* you have moved out, simply stating something like the above example I gave. But that's not even necessary because your moving out makes it clear that it's over.

Surely they will try to contact you afterward. They'll "just want to talk". But by this point, there have been hours upon hours of circular conversations that drained your life force energy. Or perhaps you've been trying to talk about things for a while, but they've been stonewalling you and avoiding those conversations. The time for talking is over and so is the relationship.

This is when blocking is very important to save yourself from the amount of pain and anguish that can come from reading their messages.

They might start sweet and sorry, but when they see you're not taking the bait, that will quickly escalate into mean and cruel. You can't unsee or unhear those words, so save yourself from the added pain by blocking them.

Do not let them know where you are or where you're going.

If it's your place and you need the narcissist to move out, this is more complicated. You may need to consult the police or an attorney for the best action plan. If you're married, this might involve offering a financial incentive for them to leave. Freedom often comes with a cost and you'll have to decide how much your freedom is worth to you.

If you have children with the narcissist, you'll need to make these decisions to move *after* getting legal counsel so you know your rights and responsibilities as a parent according to your local laws.

This is very important because if you step outside the law of your local jurisdiction, the narcissist could sue you for kidnapping, parental alienation or any number of other things.

If you have kids, your lawyer is going to be an important ally for you in this process—and likely for years to come. So be sure to find a good one. Do your due diligence and ask around for recommendations. Pay for consultations in cash so it doesn't show up on common bank accounts or credit card transactions. Hire slow and fire fast until you find one that truly understands the situation AND has the mental and spiritual cojones to take on unethical characters like this.

One tip for choosing a divorce and/or family court lawyer is to remember that you're not looking for the same qualities you would look for in a new friend or someone you'd date. You're looking for a person who is capable of being a shark in the courtroom, someone who can mentally dominate a manipulator like your ex, while also being honest, fair and direct with you.

"High conflict divorce" attorneys are often the best candidates because they are used to taking on "difficult" people. They usually don't run away from conflict or slip into fawning or people-pleasing behaviors.

If you're trying to leave a narcissistic work environment, this means quietly looking for a new job and not letting anyone in the office know. Be very careful who you're trusting in the workplace because you might not be aware that the narcissist has flying monkeys spying on you to see what you're up to.

Give your resignation notice at the latest moment permitted by your contract. Be prepared that they will try to make things very difficult from that point on and they may even try to ruin your professional reputation. You probably won't be able to count on a good job reference from that company.

Keep in mind that most corporations are toxic environments with narcissistic or psychopathic cultures, full of abusers and enablers.

If you continually find this problem everywhere you work—and if that's not the life you want—you might want to consider self-employment. Think about your experience, skills, talents and passions when you're brainstorming what you could do that adds value to people's lives and meets a need in the world so you can get paid doing it. Then look into what kinds of training you'll need in order to get that ball rolling. Working nights and weekends building a side business while you're trying to get out of a toxic work environment is a great motivation to help you focus your time and energy.

The sooner you go No Contact, the better. Every day that you stay in contact with an abuser is one more day that you're risking your health, sanity, peace, success, goals and dreams in order to maintain some semblance of a relationship.

Most people say that going No Contact was the hardest thing they've ever done.

I've even had clients who were former heroin addicts who told me that quitting heroin was easier than quitting the narcissist.

I'm not going to sugar-coat how difficult it is. However —as many people say afterward—you'll likely realize in retrospect that going No Contact was the best decision you ever made, and the only regret you have is not doing it sooner.

Once you become aware of these patterns of narcissistic abuse in one relationship, you might start to see it all around you.

If you grew up in such an environment, you'll probably find that the population density of these personality types is higher in your surroundings. That's because your nervous system was programmed to recognize abuse as love and home so you naturally gravitated toward it.

In addition, there are a lot of manipulative, abusive people out there—*way* more than the statistics will have you believing. As you start setting new boundaries with one person, you might realize that you need more boundaries with other toxic people in your life.

Once your eyes are open, it's like taking the red pill in the movie, The Matrix.

You're waking up to the fundamental crisis of humanity in modern civilization. Most people are still sleeping, so it might be lonely at first.

It's okay if others in your life can't see it yet. It's also okay if they have judgments and doubts about your awareness, your mental health and the new decisions that you're making—including the new boundaries that you're setting.

People might say things like, "you're being too picky," "you're being too hard on so-and-so," or "you should work on compassion and forgiveness."

The reality is that you're developing greater awareness and healthier boundaries—maybe for the first time in your life. You're learning to recognize the patterns of abuse and manipulation, which is not a skill that everyone has.

Each time those patterns show up, you can choose not to go down that path again, even when other people are telling you that you're wrong because they don't see it. That's part of learning and growth. As you advance in your healing process, you will outgrow some people in your life, whether they're abusers or not.

Other people may not be aware of narcissistic abuse and that's okay. Those who have never been through it (or just aren't aware of it yet) usually don't understand and often give bad advice for these situations. Be careful who you're getting advice from, even if their intentions are good. If you wanted to find a good barbecue place in town, you wouldn't ask your vegetarian friend for a recommendation because they don't know anything about that.

Others are allowed to have their opinions and those opinions don't have to define you.

What if you can't be 100% No Contact with the abuser?

These might be cases where you have kids with the narcissist so you have to have some contact in order to exchange the kids, to work out expenses or deal with illnesses and other issues or life events that come up.

This puts you in a very challenging place. By law, you will likely have to have at least one method of contact open with your ex in order to work out these details. That means you're going to have to have some contact with your ex—at least until the kids turn 18—and perhaps even afterward. For example, if they go to college, there will be financial aid forms, health insurance, expenses, etc. There will be graduations, marriages, babies and other events.

Your attorney will help you understand your local laws for dealing with co-parenting underage kids. You'll have more flexibility when they're adults. Be sure you find out what your legal rights and responsibilities are before making decisions, and be sure to have a good attorney as an important ally in this process.

In these cases where you can't be 100% No Contact, I recommend you do a modified version of No Contact. This means the very absolute, least amount of contact possible, that *only* has to do with the children and *nothing* more.

I recommend you still frame it as No Contact so you remind yourself that you're not having personal contact with your ex. This is simply a business relationship regarding the necessities and wellbeing of your children.

Don't discuss anything personal about your past relationship together. Don't share anything personal or emotional about your life. Don't react to any of their attempts to bait you into an emotional or personal conversation.

Here are some examples of what Modified No Contact is and what it isn't, to help you visualize how this will work in your life.

Examples of Modified No Contact

- You and your ex are having a conversation about the medical issue that one of your children is having. Every time your ex veers off toward personal matters, you bring the attention back to the necessary discussion of the child, simply ignoring your ex's personal comments and re-directing the conversation back to business.

- Your ex asks you to go to the amusement park with the kids together because there needs to be two adults there for when one of the kids wants to go on a ride that the other kids don't want to. You decline this invitation because that's a personal problem. If they want to go to the amusement park, they can find another adult to go with them.

- Your ex suggests you go on vacation together with the kids and stay in separate rooms. You decline this invitation because you know the boundaries of personal and business would be too blurry and you want to avoid contact.

- Your ex asks you to go together to the parent-teacher conferences. You suggest that you each split the total amount of teachers that you need to speak to. For example, if there are 8 teachers that need to be seen, your ex sees four teachers and you see a different four teachers. You both agree to email each other with a report from the teachers as a follow up.

- Your ex suggests you meet for coffee or lunch to talk about it (whatever *it* is) in person. You decline this invitation and keep the contact limited to the one channel of communication for discussing matters of the children.

- Your ex says the grandparents really want to have all the grandkids together for the holiday so they invited you and your ex to both be there since you have the kids on the holiday this year. You decline the invitation to be there and wish them a great holiday. You make other plans.

Examples of NOT being Modified No Contact

- Your ex invites you to have a cup of coffee and talk. You accept the invitation because you think *this time* you'll finally be able to work something out. Your fantasy will be your downfall.
- Your ex's family invites you both to be there for a holiday that your ex has custody for and you go because it's hard to be alone on holidays. Plus you hate that your ex gets to be with your kids for the holiday when you don't. Your loneliness will be your downfall.
- Your ex asks if you want to go on vacation with the kids together and you can have a separate hotel room. Your ex even offers to pay for everything and all you have to do is show up. You decide that you always wanted to go to the Bahamas and you deserve an all-expenses paid vacation on your ex's dime after everything you went through, so you accept the offer. Your desire for retribution will be your downfall.

- You and your ex are discussing a special performance or event that your child is doing and your ex suggests that you sit together in solidarity to cheer for your kid. You say yes thinking, that's what mature people do, right? Or maybe you agree because it would be too embarrassing for others to find out that you're going through a messy divorce or see that you're all alone. Your pride will be your downfall.

- Your ex texts you late at night to say that s/he can't pick up the kids tomorrow because something came up. You're furious, so you snap and start telling your ex that this is always what s/he does, causing these last-minute problems and emergencies, and how this really makes things difficult for you. Your resentment will be your downfall.

None of those situations will lead you anywhere good when you're dealing with a narcissist. They are traps set with enticing, emotional bait.

You'll need to become a mental ninja to manage your boundaries around Modified No Contact with your ex so you can be as healthy, clear and strong as possible for your children.

You are the lighthouse that will help your kids find the shore. If you don't keep healthy boundaries with your ex, you'll lose your light in this process. That means it's going to be really hard for your kids to find their way to solid ground from the storm at sea. Be the lighthouse and lead by example.

Keep in mind that going No Contact with abusive family members is very difficult—usually even more difficult than cutting off an intimate partner, friend, coworker or other social contact. The familial relationships are laced with layers upon layers of guilt and obligation. You might not be ready to make such a big decision yet (or ever) and that's up to you.

You can start by setting new boundaries such as declining emotional bait and other invitations that blur the line. The more you can protect your health, sanity and wellbeing the better—but as long as you're in contact, there will be inevitable harm. Eventually, you might get to the point when you realize that you have to go No Contact in order to save yourself.

Healing isn't possible until you set boundaries to minimize the damage an abusive person can do and protect your recovery process.

You can be putting in a lot of effort, doing all kinds of positive, healthy things for yourself, and trying to move forward. But if this boundary of protection is not in place, you'll continually be exposed to the abuse. You'll be on the perpetual gerbil wheel, expending a lot of energy, getting exhausted and not getting anywhere.

Then you'll get down on yourself. You'll notice pessimistic thoughts telling you that nothing will ever change despite all the work you're putting in, because you're not seeing results.

That's why you first have to protect the healing work you're doing. You will see positive results if you set the boundary of No Contact.

These are some of the many benefits of going No Contact with abusive people:

- People often describe after going No Contact (or Modified No Contact) how much better they start to feel. It's like night and day.
- The brain fog and confusion start to dissipate as you no longer have contact with the abuser.
- You'll discover a new sense of peace in your life without having to constantly deal with the abuser's attempts to hook you into another exhausting, circular conversation where they put you on the defensive.
- You'll have so much more energy for that same reason.
- Your self-esteem starts to rise. You'll notice new, positive outcomes in your life as a result of your efforts and the lack of sabotage from the abuser.
- Your self-worth increases naturally each time you set a new boundary to protect what matters to you.
- You'll start separating fact from fiction, especially regarding your sense of self, when you're no longer hearing the abuser speak false things about your character.
- You'll notice how much easier it is to own your reality when you're not exposed to the contagion of the narcissist's narrative and the hypnotic trance it induces.
- You'll be able to start taking steps forward in your healing journey without the constant setbacks of neurological hijacking caused by abuse exposure.

Keep in mind that the narcissist will hate this boundary of No Contact.

In fact, they might initially try harder to get your attention. You could think this means it's not working, but that's when you most need to *hold the line*.

They'll often become desperate to hook you back into the abuse dynamic through a conversation that starts out all lovely, then quickly turns into a nightmare. They know that if they can just get you into a conversation, the rest is easy.

Alternatively, they might take the more cowardly approach and use someone else to try to swing your perception and hook you back in. This is abuse by proxy.

Be cautious of anyone from the narcissist's network who approaches you acting concerned about you and just wanting to see how you are. They might be doing recon work for the narcissist or mining for juicy gossip for their own perverse enjoyment. The same may apply to your own family members.

Another possibility is the narcissist might initially give you the silent treatment, hoping that the punishment of rejection will pull you back in and even make *you* reach out to them.

Stand strong with your boundary and don't give in. Giving the narcissist what they want will not stop the abuse. Your compliance may give you a temporary reprieve, but the abuse will only escalate over time. That means more harm will be done in the long run.

Enforce your boundary of No Contact (or Modified No Contact) and stay strong in the face of the storm. Starve the abuser of the emotional reaction they so badly want from you.

Eventually, as you don't give any reaction whatsoever, the narcissist will stop expending energy trying to get your attention. They will move on to find an easier prey.

What happens if you don't do No Contact (or Modified No Contact)?

- You'll keep getting sabotaged and set back after every contact with the abuser.
- You'll be taking three steps forward and five steps back in your recovery journey.
- Every time you dig yourself out of the hole and go back in, it will be deeper, more painful and more difficult to get out.
- You'll be exhausted and exasperated because you're expending so much energy on managing the abuser but nothing ever gets better.
- If you leave any avenues of contact open, eventually the abuser will catch you in a moment of weakness and suck you back into the abuse dynamic.
- You'll feel worthless, like a loser or a failure, like no one else will want to love you (or whatever other lies the abuser tells you about yourself).
- Your work performance will suffer and you could run into problems with your job, business or career.
- You could lose your healthy friends because they get tired of you always complaining about the abuse while you still have contact with the abuser. They don't want to be around that energy.
- Your children will suffer because you're suffering and you won't be able to show up as the parent that you want to be for your kids.
- You'll be modeling for your children the patterns of codependency that they will likely

learn. Then they'll accept abusive people in their lives because it's what they're used to watching you do. This is one way that the Legacy of Abuse gets passed down transgenerationally.

- The amount of stress that you're going through during contact with the abuser will eventually cause you to develop health issues that rob you of your quality of life.
- You'll keep thinking that you just might be crazy.

What happens if you stay suck here?

If you set the boundary of No Contact and tell yourself that you're healed now and you're good, you will have set a very important boundary but you won't have done the inner healing work that's necessary after an abusive relationship.

After the initial relief and the positive results that you saw up until this point, eventually you'll get a gnawing feeling that something still isn't right.

You'll sense that you still don't feel as great as you hoped you would feel by now.

You might still be thinking of the abuser. You could be going in and out of fantasy, illusion, denial and false hope. You might be tempted to break No Contact because you miss the "good" parts of your abuser or the "good" times in that relationship. You could be falling into new abusers and abusive situations.

If you stay stuck here, you'll tell yourself that healing is just a matter of time but time keeps passing by and you get more frustrated because you don't feel like things are getting much better.

At any moment, the abuser could find a way to hoover you through some form of contact you weren't expecting, or perhaps casually run into you some place. They can hit just the right emotional string, and you could forget all about why you went No Contact to begin with. You could get swept back into the abuse dynamic before you even realize what happened.

That's why it's important to keep going on to the next step of the recovery process. Don't give up!

———

Step 2 Recommended Homework

How are you doing with No Contact (or Modified No Contact) right now? Cite specific examples.

Are there any ways that you're fooling yourself into thinking you're No Contact (or Modified No Contact) when you're not really?

What's the next step you can take in order to manage this boundary better?

THREE
STEP 3—RELENTLESSLY FACE THE TRUTH

Relentlessly facing the truth is now your main goal if you want to set yourself free from what happened and resolve the confusing mental torment of the cognitive dissonance.

Cognitive dissonance is what happens when your mind is trying to hold on to two opposing beliefs or thoughts. It's like a deep inner conflict.

Your mind can't reconcile these 180 degree opposing beliefs and this dissonance is very stressful. So it causes something like a short-circuit in your brain, which makes you fall back into denial. Cognitive dissonance is a coping mechanism built into the human nervous system.

Cognitive dissonance is what causes you to go back and forth in your mind like picking daisy petals . . . "s/he loves me, s/he loves me not, s/he loves me . . ."

You'll notice how in one moment you could be super lucid and clear about the fact that your ex (or other narcissist in your life) is an abuser and what you went through was abuse. Then a few minutes later you're thinking about something kind or fun that they did. Your thoughts start to tell you that maybe they're not so bad, they really do have a nice side . . . and right there, that could cause you to break No Contact before you even realize what you're doing.

The intermittent reinforcement created by the love-bombing and devaluation causes this deep mental conflict and confusion. The intermittency of the reward makes you work harder, invest more and develop an almost obsession with compliance, just to get the occasional reward.

When people question why you stayed so long, this is the reason. Your brain got addicted to the promise of the reward. This is part of the dopamine circuit.

It's the same reason people get addicted to social media. Using those platforms is like voluntarily entering into an abusive relationship.

It might look harmless initially, even exciting and fun. You aren't aware how it entices you into maintaining contact by manipulating your brain and nervous system with intermittent rewards.

But meanwhile, they're using everything you say, read, like or dislike for data mining purposes in order to extract information that will later be used against you. Your facial micro expressions are being studied in order to map your emotional reaction to stimuli. You're exposed only to the information that the abuser wants you to have access to, and the rest is silenced or smeared as disinformation. Your mind is being conditioned and programmed while your perception of reality is being curated. Yet you think you're having a good time.

Over time, you become dependent on the dopamine and develop an addiction to the promise of reward. That induces a motivational state, so you work harder to perform in order to obtain the intermittent praise. Then you crave more social validation in order to believe that you're good enough or that your feelings and perception of reality are valid.

When you become dependent on the dopamine circuit, it's difficult to leave because it feels so good. You develop an addiction. So you start to invest more in the hope of getting rewarded, and along the way, you forget how to access your critical thinking skills. You agreed to the terms and conditions without even being aware of them. You probably didn't ask enough questions or do your due diligence to investigate what you're dealing with, so you don't realize that you're being manipulated until it's too late.

It's not your fault. The human brain was wired to do this for survival. And manipulators take advantage of this, whether they're aware of what they're doing or not. What they do know is the reaction they get.

It will require grit to break free from the cognitive dissonance.

The ugly truth is hard to accept when the lie is more beautiful and it feels so much better.

In order to step into the acceptance of the truth, you'll be fighting against this survival mechanism of your human brain and nervous system. That's why the trickiest part of abuse is not leaving the abuser, but rather doing the inner work that takes place in the aftermath.

Cognitive dissonance is the first layer of the trauma bond, AKA Stockholm Syndrome or traumatic entrapment, which you'll work on breaking later in the recovery process.

Recently, I've renamed this phenomenon a Psychoneurospiritual State of Captivity. That will be the next book in this series.

This state of captivity is not based on physical confinement, however the captivity feels very real psychologically, neurologically and spiritually. It feels like there's no escape. That's why most domestic violence victims leave the house every day to go to work, take the kids to school, go to the grocery store and do life—yet they keep going home. It's an *internal* state of captivity.

In fact, a person can remain in such a state long after escaping the abusive relationship or situation.

There are 4 parameters that induce a state of captivity:

1. isolation (physical and/or psychological)
2. an act of perceived kindness (love-bombing or idealization)
3. a perceived life threat
4. a perceived inability to escape

In order for an abuser to trap a person in such a state over time, they first need to isolate the target from outside perspectives of reality.

The abuser positions themselves as the only trustworthy source of information in order to completely dominate the target's perception of reality. The target must be totally subscribed to the abuser's narrative.

Information control is reality control. This is carried out mainly through gaslighting and triangulation but also additional tactics like stonewalling, the silent treatment, smear campaigns and abuse by proxy.

Secondly, the abuser must also use intermittent acts of perceived kindness, what we call love-bombing or idealization in narcissistic abuse language.

It's not real kindness, it's just a seduction and manipulation, but the nervous system can't tell the difference. What matters is what is *perceived* as kindness. The acts of perceived kindness are alternated with acts of devaluation to create the intermittent reinforcement. Over time, this is what induces the cognitive dissonance in an abusive relationship or situation.

You've got to work on relentlessly facing the truth in order to resolve the cognitive dissonance and get your mind grounded in reality. Resolving the cognitive dissonance has to happen before you can dissolve the trauma bond. The rest of that process you'll work on later in the recovery journey.

This is how you'll train your mind to stop running the old programs that keep you stuck in denial and defensiveness. This work is like upgrading your Operating System, just like you do every so often when the manufacturer of your cellphone puts out an OS upgrade. However, this one requires your participation and effort.

How do you resolve the cognitive dissonance?

You'll need to force yourself to face the truth, all day long and every time your mind wants to remember the "good" times. Dwelling on the "good" times keeps you stuck in the cognitive dissonance and denial. This is an addictive habit that you'll need to break.

Letting yourself reminisce on what you loved about the abuser keeps you paralyzed in the inner conflict. Your brain is going to want to indulge in that fantasy because it feels much better than facing the ugly truth.

The relentless facing of the truth is how you sober up your mind from the old, addictive thought patterns leading you away from reality. You'll be working against your dopamine reward system so it's not going to feel good because it's like quitting a drug.

You'll need to practice redirecting your mind every time you catch yourself wanting to indulge in the fantasy of what it could have been, the illusion of what you thought it was, the denial of the reality in front of you, or the toxic hope that maybe things could be different.

Consistency is KEY if you want to see results.

If you do this practice inconsistently, you'll get inconsistent results. That's why I call it *relentlessly* facing the truth and not selectively or sometimes or when-you-feel-like-it facing the truth.

You must force yourself to stop using the drug if you want to get clean.

The "drug" in this case is not the abuser. It's the feeling you get when you start indulging in the fantasy, illusion, denial or toxic hope.

That feeling feels much better than the reality of the ugly truth in front of you, so naturally you would rather go there instead. However, if you want to get better and actually recover after the abuse, you'll need to force yourself to face the truth and feel the uncomfortable feelings connected to reality.

It's your choice! But there's only one way forward from here. All other paths lead backward into the repetition compulsion.

If you allow yourself to indulge in the drug—even just a taste—you are setting yourself up for an inevitable temptation and relapse. When your brain gets stuck on the "good" times, you'll likely return to the abuser or find someone very similar because it feels familiar.

One helpful practice to relentlessly face the truth is by writing the Sobriety List. This is a list of all the hurtful, mean, abusive, manipulative things that the abuser did to make you suffer since you met them. You can make a bullet-pointed list with a phrase that sums up the event or experience. I recommend writing this on paper so it's something you can touch, feel and know is real.

Every time you catch your mind wanting to indulge in the feel-good drugs that come from fantasy, illusion, denial, self-deception and toxic hope, pull out your Sobriety List. Start reading it until you snap your mind out of the trance and back into the truth and reality.

Reality is sobriety. The truth will lead you there.

In the relentless seeking of truth, you'll need to label the abuser and the abusive behavior based on what you learned in the first step during your education process. This is how you can help your mind associate a different meaning to the abuser and what happened instead of the "good" aspects you want to think about.

We talked about labels earlier in this book in Step One. You might be wondering what Step One (Educate Yourself) has to do with Step Three (Relentlessly Face the Truth) and how they're different. The first one is a mental exercise and this one is a visceral experience.

Educate Yourself is about *discovering* information.

Relentlessly Face the Truth is about *integrating* it.

Notice when your mind wants to minimize or rationalize the abuse. Reframe those behaviors for what they really are.

Do you still have a shred of hope for that relationship?

Notice the love-bombing and idealization that the abuser used to make you think that they cared or wanted the best for you. Can you see now how it was empty, superficial and hollow? Notice where in your body that

41

sensation lands. Recognize how it was all part of the abuse cycle, even though it looks nicer on the surface.

It's very common that people go in and out of denial at this stage because the brain wants to keep focusing on the "good".

By confronting the truth over and over again—and labeling things for what they are—eventually your subconscious gets on board with your conscious mind. You'll know when that spontaneous moment happens. It might be hard to explain, but you'll know that something viscerally shifted inside you and the old pull of denial is gone.

That means you've broken through the cognitive dissonance.

Eventually, further down the path of self-healing, you'll be able to look back to extract the gift and learning that you can take forward with you from the abusive relationship. However, don't worry about that right now.

In order to resolve that inner conflict and teach your brain and nervous system to stay away from the abuser, you need to understand that it was abuse and they abused you. Period.

We are not looking for redeeming qualities right now, which of course everyone has. But that level of truth is something you'll be working on later—when you'll be ready to explore more internal truths and dialectical layers of truth.

For now, you're still in Stage One of the recovery process and things are more black and white before you can restore the full color palette. Remember, one step at a time.

The truth that you'll need to integrate first is the external truth. That helps you let yourself off the hook, stop blaming yourself for what happened, and resolve the cognitive dissonance so the denial doesn't keep sabotaging your progress by hitting the repetition compulsion button.

Relentlessly facing the truth is going to help you prepare to cross the First Threshold from the powerlessness of the victim consciousness (Stage One) into the empowerment of the survivor consciousness (Stage Two). That threshold involves a commitment to self-responsibility.

For guidance through the more advanced stages of the recovery process, click here to get my book, THE JOURNEY: A Roadmap for Self-Healing After Narcissistic Abuse.

What happens if you don't relentlessly seek the truth?

- You'll keep thinking back to the "good" times at the beginning of the relationship or the abuser's "good" side, when you perceived them being kind to you.
- You won't want to think about the harm that the abuse causes. You'll minimize, normalize or otherwise rationalize it to yourself and others, like any drug addict does.
- Your mind might even delete the memories of abuse (abuse amnesia) and cause you to miss the abuser.
- You'll still be obsessed with the abuser, ruminating about them and what they're doing. At this point, your rumination will be more about hoping they can change or wondering what if you give it one more chance. You could

be thinking maybe if you just invest a little more, they'll finally realize and reciprocate.

- You might break No Contact and go back into the abuse cycle, only to start this entire process all over again.

What happens if you stay suck here at this step?

If you relentlessly face the truth about the abuser and the abuse that took place, then you can eventually resolve the cognitive dissonance, which is very important. But if you stay here, maintaining your focus solely outside yourself, you'll only be able to see the problem that the abuser has. That will keep you trapped in the powerlessness of victimhood.

You'll be unaware of the internal issues that you can work on—the patterns you need to shift—so you don't allow another relationship or situation like this in your life.

The external focus comes first but when you stop here, you'll get stuck on blaming another person, which is a very disempowered place to be. In such a state, you'll keep going through life feeling like a victim.

What other people do isn't your fault. Other people's choices and actions are entirely their responsibility. Your choices and actions are yours.

When you hear the word responsibility and feel blamed for the choices you made, that means you're still in the victim consciousness. It's normal in that stage to be unwilling or unable to take responsibility for your own choices. That just means you haven't empowered yourself yet.

It wasn't your fault and you are the only one who can do something about it now.

If you don't like your present circumstances that's okay! This means you want to change some things in your life. The next steps of transformation come from turning the focus within, shifting your own dysfunctional habits and patterns.

Your empowerment comes with the ongoing commitment to self-responsibility.

If you stay stuck here with an external focus, you'll remain disempowered. You'll continue to feel like a victim in your life. You'll keep falling into more abusers. You can end up repeating these first three steps over and over again, without moving forward.

Owning 100% self-responsibility is the challenging next step that many people never take. That keeps them returning to past abusers or accepting new abusers in their lives, continually getting hurt and further set back in the recovery process.

If you are ready to transform your life, go for it! Keep going in your self-healing even when it gets tough.

———

Step 3 Recommended Homework

Take the time to write out your Sobriety List and put it somewhere handy so you can refer to it any time you need to jolt yourself back to reality. Use bullet points to make it succinct and easy to read quickly.

FOUR

THE 3 BIGGEST MYTHS ABOUT NARCISSISTIC ABUSE RECOVERY

These are the three most common misbeliefs that people can fall into during their recovery process.

Myth 1: Learning everything you can about narcissistic abuse and the narcissist means that you're healed.

This is a myth that I often hear from people in the early stage of recovery. Unfortunately this is not true.

Education is not the same as healing. Educating yourself about narcissistic abuse is, however, a very necessary step in your healing process.

In order to change anything in your life, you first need to be aware of the problem.

Educating yourself on the phenomenon of narcissistic abuse will help you to understand what it is and what happened to you. That knowledge gives you new potential power over your life.

Knowledge becomes true power when you put it into action through the choices you make. Read that last sentence again. Write it down somewhere you can see it frequently.

It will be incredibly relieving to learn about narcissistic abuse so you can label the behavior and the narcissist. This is actually the first sense of relief that you'll have in your recovery process. You're already in a much better place than before you knew what was happening.

Don't stop here though! Remember, educating yourself is just the first step in your journey of self-healing and it's an important one.

Myth 2: Going No Contact is the same as healing.

Going No Contact is a VERY important step in the healing process but it does not equate to healing. There is still more work to be done.

No Contact is a boundary that protects your healing journey.

By setting this boundary of No Contact (or Modified No Contact), you'll be able to start taking steps forward without the constant setbacks brought on by exposure to abuse.

Myth 3: Now that I know about narcissists and narcissistic abuse, I'll never fall for this again.

This is a myth that I've seen people commenting on my videos or other social media platforms. They'll write something like, "Thanks to your videos, I now know what narcissistic abuse is and I'm healed!" Unfortunately that couldn't be farther from the truth.

The integration of this awareness is still the early stage of the journey.

Your healing process after narcissistic abuse will take time and effort. Time itself won't heal you, despite how that saying goes.

You actually have to do the work.

But what does that mean?

The work will involve radical self-care practices that you'll learn to develop in Stage Two of the recovery after narcissistic abuse. The self-care work you do is part of healing the complex post-trauma that you likely developed as a result of the abuse.

Sometimes we hear the word self-care and think spa days, mani-pedis and whatnot but that's not what I mean.

The radical self-care work involves creating an entirely new relationship with yourself by developing greater awareness of your habits and roles in relational dynamics as well as your defense mechanisms that are serving the interest of self-sabotage. It's about making new choices to restore your empowerment through reprograming your subconscious and nervous system.

The result of this ongoing, long-term inner work will also rebuild (or perhaps build for the first time in your life) self-trust, self-esteem, self-worth, self-respect and self-love.

The development of these inner qualities—and the boundaries that protect them—heals your past, restores your true essence and builds your immunity to narcissistic abuse.

CONCLUSION

Go ahead and start your recovery process by implementing the three steps you learned about in this book. I know it's daunting to think about all the work ahead of you but the sooner you begin, the sooner you'll start feeling better.

The time is going to pass by anyways. Six months from now, you'll either look back at this moment wishing you started now or feel so glad that you did.

I purposely made this material easy, simple and fast to read so you can start putting these steps into action without getting overwhelmed with too much at once.

Remember this is the *Quick Start Guide for Narcissistic Abuse Recovery*. This isn't the totality of your recovery—or even the entirety of Stage One of the self-healing process—however, these three steps will start catapulting you forward on your healing journey when you put them into action! Keep taking one step in front of the other.

Be patient with yourself—healing is a process.

Remember that consistency over time is key. If you follow these steps and you're consistent with your actions over time, you'll see positive results. The more results you see, the more motivation you'll have to keep going on the healing journey when the going gets tough.

If you're doing the work but feeling like you're not moving forward, it's very likely that you're not being consistent.

If you find yourself at that point of inertia, read through these first three steps again. Ask yourself where the chaos is getting in and where your consistency is falling short.

What happens if you don't take action? What if you read this book and then put it away and just go back to your life like nothing happened? In short, things will stay the same.

Nothing will change until you are willing to do the work to make it happen.

I know it's awful and unfair to be stuck in this situation after abuse. But it is what it is and the sooner you accept where you are, the quicker you'll be able to move forward toward where you want to be.

You are currently standing in front of a fork in your life path. You can take the easy road, which leads to a painful repetition of your past—where there is no real future since it's just all more of the same. The other option is the more challenging one, which requires work, but offers a future with much more fulfillment, joy and connection.

So ask yourself, if you keep doing what you've been doing until this point, where will you be five years from now?

Where does that road lead?

What will be the cost?

How much more of yourself will you lose on that path?

If you never start the healing journey, things will only

get worse. You might even get sick or lose your mind from all the stress. When I've worked with clients who were in decades-long abusive relationships, they all had one or more chronic illnesses.

You can stay stuck, dwelling on the unfairness and resentments. You can refuse to take responsibility for your life. You can keep going along as you have been. But none of that will change anything. It's your choice how you respond to your life experiences. Choose wisely.

I hope this *Quick Start Guide to Recovery After Narcissistic Abuse* helped you to get on the entrance ramp to the highway of your self-healing journey.

It's not easy to restore yourself after a narcissist has rampaged your life. When it started in childhood, the work is even more challenging.

I also know that it's totally worth the effort you invest in your recovery. Along the way, you'll discover just how strong, resilient and amazing you are. It takes grit, and you can do it!

RECOMMENDED RESOURCES

Here are some books, videos and podcast episodes I recommend for you to delve further into the recovery process after narcissistic abuse.

Books

- *People of the Lie* (Dr. M. Scott Peck)
- *Psychopath Free* (Jackson MacKenzie)
- *The Sociopath Next Door* (Dr. Martha Stout)
- *Why Does He Do That?* (Lundy Bancroft)
- *In Sheep's Clothing* (Dr. George Simon)
- *The Gift of Fear* (Gavin DeBecker)
- *The Journey: A Roadmap for Self-healing After Narcissistic Abuse* (Meredith Miller)
- *The Covert Passive-Aggressive Narcissist* (Debbie Mirza)

Videos from Inner Integration on YouTube

- 5 Ways to Disarm Toxic People
- Responding vs. Reacting | How to Avoid the Narcissist's Trap
- Responding vs. Reacting | Next Level
- Gaslighting
- You Know You're In Narcissistic Abuse When...
- 6 Keys to Build Immunity to Narcissistic Abuse
- Don't Give Your Power Away to the Narcissist (or other toxic person)

- Overcoming Loneliness After Narcissistic Abuse
- Self-Sabotage After Narcissistic Abuse
- Leaving a Narcissist Before the Discard

Podcast Episodes from Inner Integration on iTunes, Stitcher or Spotify

- Resolving the Cognitive Dissonance from Narcissistic Abuse
- Cognitive Dissonance & Trauma Bonding
- No Contact: Taking Your Power Back and Protecting Your Peace
- The Narcissistic Abuse Cycle
- Why Is Love-Bombing So Dangerous?
- The 4 Pillars of Recovery After Narcissistic Abuse
- When You're Hoping Someone Will Change
- Codependency Caused By Abuse
- Leaving the Narcissist
- Boundaries: Setting Limits with Manipulative People
- Complex PTSD After Abusive Relationships
- Reactive Abuse Will Get You In Trouble
- C-PTSD After Abusive Relationships
- The Danger of the Fantasy

ABOUT THE AUTHOR

Meredith Miller is a holistic coach, author, and speaker who helps people self-heal after narcissistic abuse and other toxic relationships. Her mission is to bridge the gap between trauma and purpose. She teaches mindsets and tactical tools to help with recovery and empower people to transform their lives after abuse. Meredith's holistic coaching lens is a valuable complement to traditional psychotherapy.

www.InnerIntegration.com

ALSO BY MEREDITH MILLER

THE JOURNEY

A Roadmap for Self-healing After Narcissistic Abuse

Made in the USA
Monee, IL
22 July 2024

62504110R00046